Cherries

-JUST RIGHT!

by **Jennifer Johnson**
illustrations by **Anja Jonsson**

FriesenPress

Suite 300 - 990 Fort St
Victoria, BC, V8V 3K2
Canada

www.friesenpress.com

Copyright © 2017 by Jennifer Johnson
First Edition — 2017

Illustrations by **Anja Jonsson**

www.littlecherriesontheprairie.com

ISBN
978-1-4602-9956-2 (Paperback)
978-1-4602-9957-9 (eBook)

1. *JUVENILE NONFICTION, LIFESTYLES, FARM & RANCH LIFE*

Distributed to the trade by The Ingram Book Company

Dedication

This book is lovingly dedicated to my husband, my first love, who so patiently and gently walks alongside me and all my crazy ideas. I love you, Dwayne!

Testimonials

"This book does a good job of portraying the typical growing cycle and season of sour cherries, with all of the risks and rewards that come to producers and their families."
—ROBERT SPENCER, Horticulturist

"Being the Johnson family's Homeschool Teacher Consultant for the past eleven years, I've grown to love and respect Jennifer's dedication and commitment to her family, church, and community. Her cherry book is a must-read, and an excellent *conversation* book for the living room coffee table."
—CAROL PURVES, teacher

Cherries

were Abi's favourite fruit.
They were sweet and red,
and they could be

SQUEEZED

into the best juice she
could put in her mouth.

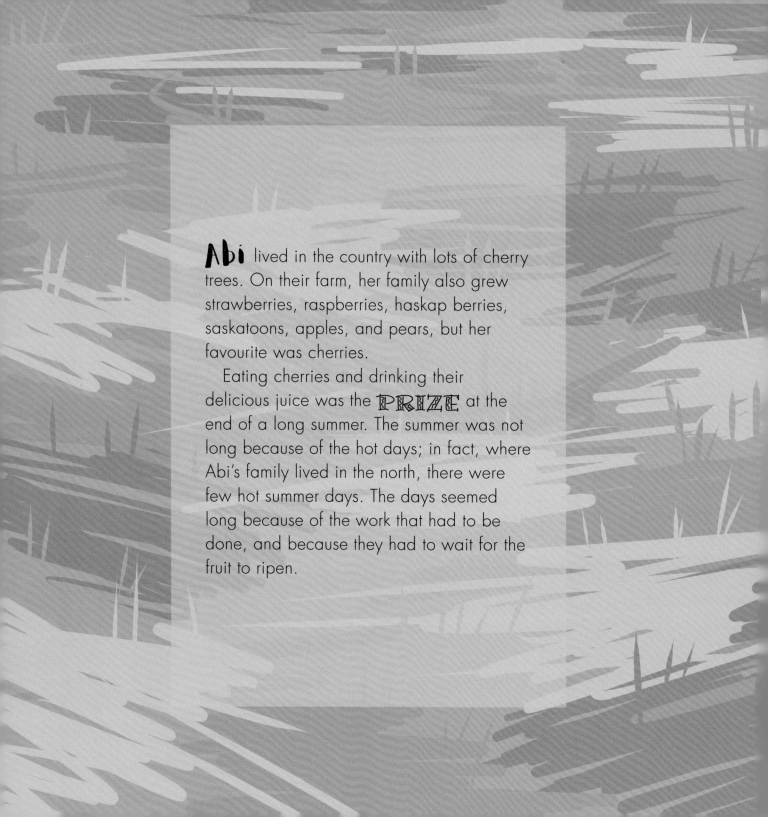

Abi lived in the country with lots of cherry trees. On their farm, her family also grew strawberries, raspberries, haskap berries, saskatoons, apples, and pears, but her favourite was cherries.

Eating cherries and drinking their delicious juice was the PRIZE at the end of a long summer. The summer was not long because of the hot days; in fact, where Abi's family lived in the north, there were few hot summer days. The days seemed long because of the work that had to be done, and because they had to wait for the fruit to ripen.

Spring brought cherry **BLOSSOMS,** the prettiest sight in the country!

With those blossoms came the promise of fruit and the beginning of a new season.

By summertime, the blossoms had swollen into little green marbles, and our work began. Weeds had grown and needed to be pulled. Newly planted trees still needed water if the rains held off. Fabric and bark mulch were laid down around rows.

THERE WAS A JOB FOR EVERYONE, AND THE FAMILY WORKED TOGETHER.

To pass the time, Abi's older brothers would get creative. Josh, the oldest, ever the **IMPERSONATOR**, began to quote radio personalities. From the financial advisor ("Where debt is dumb and cash is king, and the paid-off home mortgage has taken the place of the BMW . . .") and the music station ("This is Ronnie Max and Bethany Nicole bringing you this weekend's top twenty!"), and of course the kids' shows with altered voices ("Sully, stop hitting that warthog on the head, or you will end up ruining a perfectly good coconut!").

Caleb, Abi's next oldest brother, was usually **LAUGHING** by the time Josh started impersonating a giraffe, and most certainly by the time he was squeaking out monkey noises! If the minutes ever began to drag by in silence and boredom, Caleb would quietly ask Josh a leading question to get him to once again pick up the impersonations and keep the laughter going.

Luke was the youngest of the three brothers, and the most **NAIIVE**.

As the cherries began to turn pink, and before the sweetness of the dark red appeared, inevitably Caleb would convince Luke to eat at least one of those sour pink cherries. Luke's face would pucker up, his eyes would squint shut against the tang, and Caleb would again burst into laughter. With the unripe fruit still in his mouth, Luke would still manage to smile. Realizing he had been conned yet again, he grinned and even managed a small giggle.

Eventually, those sour pink cherries turned a rich, dark crimson. With each passing day, the colour grew darker and the SUGARS INSIDE became sweeter, and it was almost time to pick them.

"Three more days!" declared Mom after a walk-through and inspection of the orchard.

"YAY!" exclaimed Abi, not fully understanding that in order to eat the delicious fruit and drink their sweet juice, the family would have to spend hours and days picking and sorting them!

"Nooooo," groaned Luke, who fully understood the work that lay ahead.

Mom simply smiled at each of their reactions, and then she went to make sure there would be enough pails ready for the job. Finding and cleaning the pails took up most of the day.

Heavy air greeted them all the next morning. The day was unusually hot by the time breakfast was over, and by lunchtime they had all moved into the basement to cool down. It would be an afternoon of organizing and cleaning the basement—and perhaps playing some games, as well—to escape the scorching heat.

"Well," said Mom, "at least we'll get some much-needed organizing done, and with this heat, those cherries might just be ready to PICK TOMORROW!"

The air outside grew even hotter as the afternoon wore on, and by suppertime, dark clouds were billowing ACROSS the sky.

Approaching quickly, they were black, churning, and threatening. Supper waited as anxious eyes peered through the window, hoping for the best, yet wondering about the worst.

Light flashed on the horizon, followed by a distant, low rumble. Lightning approached, increasing in brilliance, always followed by a crescendo of thunder. Spits of rain began to FALL, growing into a larger and harder downpour. Within seconds, the rainstorm turned into an icy destruction; hail beat down everything in its path. Balls of ice the size of grapes pounded the ground. The noise was deafening, and each face that was watching reflected the terror of the STORM.

It was over as quickly as it had started. However, even though the storm had ended, it had brought with it the beginning of a new stage; clean-up and repairs would now be needed on the farm to put things back in order and fix what had been broken.

Diamonds sparkled on the fresh, clean grass, as steam rose off the front walk in the crisp air, and everything SHONE from the recent shower. The freshness of the air and sparkling purity masked the terrible damage that had been done.

"Well," said Dad, "who's coming for a walk with me?"

"I will," said Abi.

"Me too," agreed Luke.

Mom smiled her willingness as well, and the entire family put on their rubber boots and jackets to go for their walk, knowing that Dad had really meant they were going to inspect the hail's destruction.

"Mom, will there be any cherries left?" asked Abi.

"We'll see," responded Mom. Losing this cherry crop would mean no extra fruit in the freezer for the winter, and nothing to sell to their faithful customers.

walking to the orchard revealed broken tree branches,

PILES OF HAIL,

19 and battered leaves.

Cherries littered the ground in the orchard, covering it like a blanket. Everyone's face was solemn, recognizing the great loss.

"At least we have some strawberries and raspberries in the freezer," said Abi, trying to be brave.

Mom smiled. "That's right, Abi," she said.

"THERE'S ALWAYS SOMETHING THAT WE CAN BE GRATEFUL FOR."

Dad had been quiet. He was gently moving branches around and slowly walking down one row of trees.

"Abi, come and look," he said, parting the branches of one tree and exposing the interior.

Abi eased eased forward, her disappointed eyes sad yet curious. Peeking into the tree, her face instantly BRIGHTENED, and she smiled from ear to ear.

"CHERRIES!"

she exclaimed with delight.

Deep inside those trees, protected by the branches and leaves, were beautiful dark-red cherries, many of them bruised and battered but still HANGING from their determined stems. Popping one in her mouth, Abi bit down, letting the sweet juices run down her throat.

"IT'S JUST RIGHT!" she declared, reaching for another one.

Heat from the day and the cooling rain had really intensified the flavour and made those remaining cherries "just right."

"You know," said Mom, "most of the cherries might be lost on the ground, and the ones left on the trees are rather bruised and not fit for freezing or drying, but I think there might be enough left here to provide some juice for the coming winter."

With those words, everyone's mood lifted. The resulting GRATITUDE—perhaps intensified by the recent emotions the storm had caused—brought a spirit of celebration. Dad, Mom, and Abi laughed and chatted as they searched for untouched fruit to nibble on. The boys would have been doing the same if they hadn't been so distracted by the arsenal of dropped fruit on the ground, tempting them to a cherry fight.

"No matter what comes our way, it can always be worse, and we can always find something for which to be thankful," said Dad. He popped a cherry in his mouth, and then another one came

WHIZZING

over from the battle behind him,
splattering on the back of his head.

Abi giggled, POPPED a cherry in her mouth, and began looking for another. She loved having all of her family together, and her smile revealed her joy in having cherries that were just right!

Printed in Canada